Corn Likker & Daffodils

poems by

Eve Hoffman

Finishing Line Press
Georgetown, Kentucky

Corn Likker & Daffodils

For Sal

Making art is my way of making sense of the world.

Copyright © 2025 by Eve Hoffman
ISBN 979-8-89990-024-2 First Edition
All rights reserved under International and Pan-American Copyright Conventions. No part of this book may be reproduced in any manner whatsoever without written permission from the publisher, except in the case of brief quotations embodied in critical articles and reviews.

Also By Eve Hoffman

Memory & Complicity

SHE

Red Clay

A Celebration of Healing

Listening to the Struggle

Publisher: Leah Huete de Maines
Editor: Christen Kincaid
Cover Art: Judith Hoffman
Cover Photographer: Sal Brownfield
Author Photo: Sal Brownfield

Order online: www.finishinglinepress.com
also available on amazon.com

Author inquiries and mail orders:
Finishing Line Press
PO Box 1626
Georgetown, Kentucky 40324
USA

Contents

PREFACE xi

THE RECIPE 1

BEYOND MY DISHWATER HANDS 3

IN MY BASEMENT THE STUFFED RED FOX 4

WHAT TO BELIEVE 5

AT THE GEORGIA STATE FAIR 6

NIGHT RIDE IN A 1954 GREEN AND WHITE CHEVY 8

DOUBLE HELIX 11

MY MOTHER TAUGHT ME TO NAME PLANTS 13

(UNTITLED) 16

WITNESS 17

A CLIMATE OF DENIERS 20

INTRODUCTIONS 23

THIRTEEN YEARS OLDER 24

EIGHT YEARS A WIDOW 25

THE ARTIST BREWS EARLE GRAY TEA 26

LIGHTS 28

INTERMISSION 29

METAMORPHOSIS 30

THE CARIBOU ACCORDS 32

YOUR EYEBROWS PRAISE DANDELIONS 34

THE GATHERING	36
INSURRECTION JANUARY 6	38
VULCANUS ERUPTUS	41
ON VISITING AN ABECEDARIAN ATELIER	42
CAST IRON SKILLETS	44
NEELY FARM	45
PICK-UP STICKS	48
ALONG BUCK CREEK	49
SEVEN DAYS IN SPRING	51
MELANCHOLIA COVIDA	53
CONTAGION	54
THROUGH THE LENS OF DORTHEA LANGE'S CAMERA	56
FOG	57
PETITION	58
CATCHING AIR BEFORE THE SHOALS	59
TREE	60
NOTES	64
ACKNOWLEDGMENTS	65
EVE HOFFMAN	66

As wave is driven by wave
And each, pursued, pursues the wave ahead,
So time flies on and follows,
flies, and follows,
Always, forever and new. What was before
is left behind; what never was is now;
And every passing moment is renewed.

Ovid, Metamorphoses 8 CE

Preface

Corn Likker & Daffodils. Eve Hoffman invites us into the back seat of the family car watching the KKK cross the street. She is seven. At sixteen her Atlanta synagogue is bombed. As a grandmother she watches torches snake down the steps in Charlottesville. We join her at the Georgia State Fair. Carousel horses, blue ribbons for 4-H calves and cotton candy laced with lies. Personal and political not always separate. She takes us to the 1930s eroded Georgia red clay her grandfather turned into a prize winning dairy farm. We hear earthmovers carve fertile fields and verdant pastures into streets. We stand beside twenty-foot roots of trees on a clear-cut hill. Gone, the smell of fresh cut hay and manure. We watch a five hundred year Chattahoochee flood come within two hundred yards of her kitchen. We join her great-grandmother putting on suffragette sash. We are at the bedside as her husband dies and on a hillside when grandchildren pick daffodils he planted forty years before. We are with her, a widow of eight years, when friends "set her up" with an artist. She walks us along Buck Creek after storms. A chaos of limbs, yellow tennis balls, new eddies and beaches. We come upon a shed covered in hate graffiti. We learn as her mother teaches her to name plants—bloodroot and trillium and as another mother teacher her daughter to name plants as they cross the desert—lupines and giant saguaro. We share with Eve Hoffman a cup of "medicine" her five-year old granddaughter mixes in a galvanized bucket. *It will heal everything.*

Paul Wolpe, Founding Director, Emory University Center for Peacebuilding and Conflict Transformation

The Recipe

Granddaughter
making medicine
in a
galvanized
bucket
dented
dirt
pebbles
soft green grass
Japanese maple
seedlings
volunteers
rosemary
thyme
leek flowers
brown leaves
water
a sturdy stick
for blending
It's like tangled hair
like pasta
kelp
you have to pull it up
while stirring
she sniffs it
pours some into
pottery

a small blue
cup
brings it to me
It will heal everything.

Beyond My Dishwater Hands

a ruby-throated hummingbird drinks from red
Egyptian star cluster blossoms, moves on
to yellow lima bean flowers. Nineteen *ballet*

slipper hibiscus blossoms, fragile white petals,
ruffled pale pink edges, dinner plate size. I dry
my hands, go out to measure. Seven inches

across. Deep center red stain seeps up partway.
Two-inch pistil and stamen, yellow filaments
end in dots erotic as any Georgia O'Keefe

painting. Bumblebee legs weighted in layers
of pollen defy gravity, take flight. Squirrels
fly from a post holding the hibiscus, leap four

feet past the baffle to the bird feeder.
Others trench under caging protecting beef-
steak tomatoes, leave a half-eaten one balanced

on top of a tomato stake, another twenty
yards away on the limb of a Chinese Fringe
tree too high for us to reach. Others chase

one another, upend potted begonias and inpatients,
cut holes in netting over a twenty-foot fig tree.
Black snake caught in the netting. We find it dead.

In My Basement the Stuffed Red Fox

    my grandfather shot on his Georgia
dairy farm/ a photograph of him holding
the dead fox/ I'd watch him lift the blued-
barrel, polished smooth walnut stock
of his Remington 12 gauge shotgun/
release the safety, yell *pull*/ clay pigeons
take flight, explode mid-air/ spent shells
kick to the ground/ smell of burnt gunpowder,
sulfur, metallic/ he reloads after each
shot/ sights a dove in season, a copper-
head or rabid fox anytime.

l learn to shoot a 4-10 shotgun at summer
camp/ along with canoeing, horseback riding,
and braiding lanyards/ standing or prone steady
the aim at black concentric circles on paper
targets/ release the safety, squeeze the trigger
gently/ spent shells kick to the ground/
reload after each shot/ I earn three NRA
safety badges/ *Treat all guns as loaded/
Always keep guns pointed towards the ground.*

Today I can order on the internet/an AK-47
assault weapon / six hundred rounds per minute,
six hundred dollars/ a pink one for my grand-
daughter who finds the fox in the basement
dusty and creepy/ her male cousins ask
Can we take it home?

What to Believe

What to believe this winter day
of *life after death*—
a warm muffled sewing room

rows of narrow tables

wrapped in unbleached muslin
a single light bulb hangs
from the ceiling over each table

women

in dark ankle-length dresses
long white bibb aprons
bend over the muslin-wrapped tables

their fingers

soothe shards of sinew and skin
with stitches of fine thread. As final
knots are tied off, stitches begin to fade

girls and boys of six and seven

sit up, stand up on the muslin tables
wearing outfits chosen for school pictures,
hair brushed, faces scrubbed
this day in Sandy Hook.

At the Georgia State Fair

On the summer breezes French fries, corn dogs,
cattle barns where 4-H kids parade hoped-for prize-

winning calves. Funnel cakes compete with Marie
Antoinette pastries laced with champagne conspiracies.

I climb on my red & pink carousel horse, impatient
for the calliope to signal we're about to move. Carnival

barkers hawk Jonestown Kool Aid, hand out tickets
to the Kiss-the-Dear-Leader's-Ring booth. In the

Scientific Method tent tidy rows of glass boxes display
a two-headed calf, a *genuine* mermaid, testicles

& vertebrae of elected officials. I catch up with my
brothers spinning red lunch counter stools, ordering

grilled cheese sandwiches & Coke Cola. We watch
little girls become princesses after their turn in

the face-painting booth. Uncle Sam on stilts catches
a balloon escaping a four year old wrist. Pre-teen

boys & girls sneak first kisses behind Midway tents
Cotton candy machines spin pink & blue lies. I wait

my turn to knock down *swimming* ducks with a red
ball, win a key ring with a tiny yellow fuzzy duck.

Neon orange arrows direct fairgoers into a Congress
of concave mirrors where a Texas Senator inveighs

in Joseph McCarthy cadence. Blue ribbons hang
beside 4-H pigs & sheep to be sold for breeding

or butchering. Fireworks signal the fair is closing
for the night. Lights flicker off barns of with chickens

& turkeys, goats & shoats, tables of jams & jellies. The Ferris
Wheel blinks dark. In carnie caravans contracts

for liquor, cards & whores are settled. The soles
of my new red Keds sticky with popcorn & cotton

candy collect parking lot gravel. In my pocket a tiny
yellow fuzzy duck. From the backseat of the car I plead

with my brothers. *Do we really have to listen to the Atlanta
Crackers baseball game the whole hour-long ride home?*

Night Ride in a 1954 Green and White Chevy

Summer night. Full moon shadows. Sixteen year old girl driving twenty miles home from downtown Atlanta to rural Norcross.
> *Just five more miles to go. I can loosen the sweaty grip on my steering wheel.*

Gas tank full. Doors locked. Windows rolled up. Right turn from Winters Chapel onto Spalding. Radio off.
> *I promised Momma no radio until I'd had my driver's license three months.*

Headlights come fast up behind me. A pickup truck swerves past. Muffler blasting. Boys shouting catcalls. Slows to 15 MPH at my bumper.
> *I slam brakes to the floorboards.*
> *Are they trying to get me to hit them?*

Warm summer night. Two lane country road. Girl just sixteen driving alone. Boys joy-riding. Whoopin' and whistlin'.
> *I know this road. I can pass the truck. Leave three car lengths between us as taught.*

Again. High and low beams flash in my rearview mirror. Pickup speeds around me. Swallows three car lengths. Slows to 15 MPH .

> *What kind of game are they playing? I'm almost home, I can pass them one more time.*

And again. Headlights blinking, closing in on my rearview mirror. Horn blasting. The truck swings past. Holds at 15 MPH at my bumper.

> *Ignore them. Only half mile until my final turn. Do not try to pass them! Do not use the turn signal!*

Last rise in the road home. 15 MPH. Caravan. Pickup truck of rowdy boys followed by a sixteen year old girl in a green and white 1954 Chevy.

> *Ease my foot off the gas. Get ready to turn left onto the gravel road. I look up.*

The pickup keeps going past my turn. Keeps on going. Keeps on going.

> *Hard left turn. Wheels spin into the crunch of gravel. Burn of rubber. Only the summer dust follows me home.*

Double Helix

In my olive skin and deep red lips
Abram Alexander
descendant of fourteenth century
Jewish intellectuals
who escape the Spanish Inquisition
2nd LY in the American Continental Army.

In the angle of my cheekbones
Leopold Schlesinger
Jewish bodyguard of Emperor Franz Joseph
distinguished soldier of the Austrian Army
His wife Nettie, a Hungarian gypsy,
in the slope of my child-bearing pelvis.

In the hazel of my eyes
Lottie Ritz (Papilsky) Parker
arrives at Ellis Island from The Pale circa 1900
braids challah, reads the Yiddish newspaper
two sons American Colonels
wounded in World War II.

In the femur of my legs Irish lad
Benjamin Neely
stows away on a ship to Cuba. Civil War double agent,
1884 Georgia school superintendent builds
a school for *colored* children equal to that for white ones.

In the bend of my elbows and knees
J.J. Cohen German-born proprietor
of a Georgia mercantile store and mill
hangs near to death
as Yankee scalawags dig up his backyard
searching for the family silver.

In my voice Ella Cohen Schlesinger
Secretary of the Georgia Equal Suffrage Party
jailed marching for my right to vote
third great-grandmother of my daughter
jailed in Chicago protesting
America's run-up to the 2003 war into Iraq.

In my pearl earrings Rae Schlesinger Neely
drafts Georgia adoption and education standards,
critiques manuscripts for New York publishers
teaches a grandson math
using New York Times box scores.

In my hands Rachel Neely Parker picks daffodils
and tulips, introduces me to Aida's
Triumphal March, Rachel Carson's *Silent Spring*
Masters of Social Work in her fifties
at sixty-seven her heart stops during hip surgery
she survives thirteen years
absent her gifts of intellect and finding
four-leaf clovers. My mother.

My Mother Taught Me to Name Plants

roadsides and ditches of thistle   and golden tickseed
blue cornflowers and   purple vetch   taught me
to return smiles   to velvet pansy faces   to blow on
dandelions gone to seed to pull daisy petals one
at a time *He loves me /loves-me-not*   She taught
me   lavenders dilly-dally   sultanas grow impatient
dragons snap to attention   when four-o-clocks
toll   ladies slip home late   and Jack preaches from
his pulpit of golden chanterelles and trillium   She
taught me to listen for the crack of antlers as white
tail buck spar   not to be afraid of five foot black
king snakes   who eat rats and copperheads nor
of the crack of lightening   not to be terrified
by the chilling call of a tiny screech owl or packs
of baying hounds treeing racoons on full moon
nights   not to fear the river rising from its bend
flooding bottomlands   She taught me to eavesdrop
on the breath of iris, tulips and daffodils   on the
whisper of spring on woodland hills of bloodroot
and mayapple   She taught me listen for the rattling
trumpet of   a sedge of sandhill cranes   migrating
five thousand feet overhead   silence of a box
turtle resting in the middle of a road   She taught
me to find four-leaf clovers   to avoid poison ivy
not to eat pokeweed   holly berries or foxglove   She
taught me to find Ursa Major cradling the Big
Dipper in night skies   She taught me the sweetness
of jasmine and gardenia   the kindness of Susan
tending the black eye

                              of a girl in a cage
                              on America's doorstep

whose own mother had taught her to name plants
lupines paloverde purslane resurrection which
survives   extreme drought   and Spanish
missionaries used to preach resurrection   She
taught her   daughter to read the arroyos   mesas
mudflat playas   to name organ pipe   hedgehog
barrel and pincushion cactus   She welcomed
her daughter into   sanctuaries of giant saguaro
where gilded flickers and gila woodpeckers drill
nesting holes   taught her   swallowtail sulphur
and gossamer winged butterflies   mariposa de
noche and white sphynx tiger   nocturnal moths
She taught her to listen for swarms of bees gathering
nectar and pollen   in poppy fields   for lizards
scampering rocks   and for the thunder of prowling
male bobcats in mating season   She taught her
daughter   cleansing power of white sage   and
passion flower and medicinal properties   of desert
lavender and prickly pear   taught her   to make
acedia echinacea and brittle bush tea   taught her
the deadly properties of nightshade   red spotted
caps of fly agaric mushrooms   She taught her
the disposition of two and of four legged coyotes
temperament the of diamond back rattlesnakes She
taught her the soul of the Rio Grande   archeology

of abandoned migrant rest stops   threadbare
backpacks   dried up worn diapers and   children's
sandal   taught her daughter to sign the cross when
passing bodies and bones in desert scorch and
to pray remembrance for their nameless souls
on the Day of the Dead   She taught her daughter
songs of the North Star   and in the rainy season
they cartwheeled together   across desert pastures
of wildflower bloom.

(Untitled)

Two descriptions of Sal Brownfield's 60" x 48" oil and shellac painting

Dark hair falls behind her shoulders, her thin right arm thrusts up fierce through the wide glossy-black brushstroke half height of the five-foot canvas. Tendons and muscles in her arm stretched smooth, plow hell-rains of reds, yellows and oranges. Her elbow a flat plane hovers through black spaghetti-drip curtains, arches and arcs. Her face follows her fist assaulting the cobalt sky. Ear bruised. Neck muscles rigid. Tear-seared cheek. Her jaws lock open as in Guernica. She keens. *We will not be silent!* She howls. *We will not all be murdered!* Her eyes, obsidian holes of fear.

~ ~ ~

Dark hair falls behind her shoulders, tendons and muscles in her right arm unfold, elbow opens near double-jointed. Her fist traces the wide vertical black brushstroke half-height of the five-foot canvas, skips past black arcs, arches, curtains of black spaghetti. Her thin arm sails yellow currents, shoals of orange as she reaches into cloudless blue. Face skyward. Her dark eyes flood with relief. Jaws slack, gather salt tears. She falls to her knees, *Jesus! Jesus!* Signs the cross over her face, back and forth across her chest. *Gracias Jesus! Jesus Gracias!*

Witness

I am seven years old.
Men in white robes, holes for eyes in peaked hoods, cross the road in front of us, climb into the back of a large white box truck. I dream for weeks they will come take me and my family away in that white truck. We are Jewish.

I am twelve.
Ralph McGill, 1950s-60s publisher of the *Atlanta Constitution*, writes front page editorials condemning segregation. From his front porch Mr. McGill shows me where the Ku Klux Klan burns crosses in his yard.

Sixteen.
I become President of the Temple Youth Group. Four hours later the Temple is bombed.

Forty.
Elected member of the Gwinnett Board of Education. We deny the KKK use of the high school parking lot across a two-lane road from their nighttime rally.

Fifty-nine.
Without Sanctuary exhibit. 100+ photos and postcards of lynchings. I did not know Blacks were hung in courthouse yards, from telephone poles, bridges. Bodies burned and beaten, four or five hung from the same tree. 10,000+ whites attend, bring their children.

Sixty-six.
I translate the plaque on a Paris school wall. *From 1942 to 1944 more than 11,000 children were deported from France …assassinated in the death camps simply because of being born Jewish. We will never forget them.* I realize for the first time my mother was pregnant with me as these children are murdered.

Sixty-seven.
Our friend Eva and her mother escaped the Nazis. On the way to her Georgia memorial service a battered pick-up truck passes. American flag on the rusted passenger door, bumper sticker reads *I will forgive Jane Fonda when the Jews forgive Hitler.*

Seventy-six.
Men and some women in Khaki pants and white polo shirts light torches, fall in line two-by-two, snake down University of Virginia campus steps. Spit flies from their screaming mouths. *Blood and Soil. Jews will not replace us! Jews are Satan's children*

The following morning.
Stakeholders in a white American ethno-state reassemble. Confederate Stars and Bars, swastikas. Call and response. *One people! White pride!* Fists and arms land on counter-protesters. Six white men beat a Black man with pipes and boards. *Go the fuck back*

to Africa! A Dodge plows into counter-protesters. Bodies tossed airborne. Thirty-five injured. Para-legal Heather Heyer is murdered. I walk out my kitchen door into the familiarity of Georgia heat and humidity

Coda

Four days later President Trump breaks his silence. *There are very fine people on all sides! You had a group on the other side that was also very violent. Very fine people on all sides.*

A Climate of Deniers

Tip of the hat to James Lipton An Exaltation of Larks

A climate of deniers
a conception of personhoods
a placenta of birthers
a closet of homophobes
a frenzy of sycophants
a trench of conspirators
a vanity of obstructionists
a legacy of voter suppressors
a virus of ideologues
a cloak room of toadies
a gangrene of trumpters
a mire of incompetents
a ditch of bigots
a perfidy of tyrants
a gallery of fear-mongers
a cache of dark monies
the silence of enablers

Introductions

He introduces my five-generation Georgia family
to bear hugs and laughter. Introduces me to the
Redwoods of Muir Woods, crashing waves and kelp
forests of Big Sur. He bounds off the Powell /Hyde
Street Cable car, skips the line at Swenson ice cream,
buys a vanilla cone, leaves the change, chases
the cable car up the hill, jumps back on, hands me
the cone to the cheers of other riders. He straps me
to the deck of a Tahiti Ketch sailing under the Golden
Gate Bridge and south in the Pacific for Monterey.
Sea-sickness is real! He tosses cabers in the California
Highland games. Surprises me with a six-week old
Newfoundland puppy hidden in his jacket on a flight
from New York to San Francisco. He takes me to the
ski slopes of Yosemite, adjusts my bindings, leaves me
on the bunny hill, heads for the black diamond trails.
We sell our bed, our tables and chairs, pack a U-Haul
and our puppy, drive across the southern United
States to the Georgia farm where I grew up. He clears
land and builds our home. Hammers and nails, skill saws
and roofing tacks. Joins heart-cut boards of a loblolly pine
he had to take down into a seventeen foot dining table.
Remains confident I will become pregnant even
after a California doctor advised my fallopian tubes
were blocked. We register for childbirth classes.
He holds our son and two daughters as they take first
breaths and first steps. Tells them night-time stories

of the *Tweedie-Dum-Dinkums* sometimes falling asleep before they do. *Mom! Daddy snores. Can we tape him?* He buys our children sausage biscuits wrapped in cellophane at Nalley's gas station, heats them in a microwave I am convinced leaks radiation. He encourages me to run for the Board of Education. When he runs for public office swastikas are painted on his signs. He is branded *a communist* advocating protection of the Chattahoochee River and its state-wide water supply. He takes our eight year-old son to the Rose Garden when President Jimmy Carter signs federal legislation protecting the river. He cheers for every kid at soccer games. *Dad, you really don't need to cheer for the other team, especially when they are winning.* He sings in a Barbershop chorus, plants a field daffodils.

Thirteen Years Older

Did he worry about becoming *really old first?* Becoming a burden? I promised before we stood under the chuppah that July scorching Georgia afternoon to never leave him tethered to wires, tubes, beeps and blinking lights. *If necessary tip me in my wheelchair over a cliff.* Did he imagine me a widow at fifty-one—hazel eyes memorizing milestones in our children's lives. Broken arms and broken hearts. Bar and Bat Mitzvahs, college applications, graduations, weddings. Did he imagine me sharing with yet-to-be-born grandchildren stories of Grandpa Howard—himself a prodigious storyteller, no need to exaggerate. Did he see me remembering to take out the garbage on Thursday nights, cutting a chicken breast in half, freezing part. My grocery basket —six eggs, three apples, a quart of 2 % milk. No half and half.

Eight Years a Widow

I.
Doors close, silence
London, Paris, Barcelona

map locations, not memories
locked windows deny

passageways to the soul's attic
forswear panic into pleasure

muffled sounds slip 'round corners
it is difficult to breathe

II.
Wisp of air safe and risk-filled
mushroom risotto, a candle

doors fling wide open
test threshold of their hinges

windows loosen their frames
into the soul's attic a Zuni

fetish necklace, warm strawberry fields
robin spring song, first daffodils.

The Artist Brews Earle Gray Tea

   … in his studio, comes for a spring walk
along the river near my home. In the front hall

he picks up a snapshot from the large Wedgewood
bowl—a man holding the bowl. *He must have*

laughed a lot! Shivers settle down on my eight-
years-a-widow shoulders. *How can it be a man*

I've only recently met knows this about my late
husband of twenty-eight years? We walk past

shoals, centenarian oaks, mountain laurel about
to bloom. Under sycamores in a meadow he

puts a hand on my shoulder, stops me. *Sshhh*
hush. (Not something I'm used to being told.)

How many different birdsongs do you hear?
We trace Georgia dirt roads alongside ditches

of purple vetch, blue bachelor buttons, summer
cacophony of crows, cicadas and frogs. Catch

whiting in the Atlantic surf. He stirs mushroom
risotto in his studio. I chop eggplant and zucchini

for ratatouille in my kitchen, find candles. He opens
a Pinot. I hold my stomach in a little tighter.

I begin to write poetry. A scrum of forgotten feelings.
Phrases fumble, clauses seek ground. Raw stanzas.

The artist stretches canvas for *A Celebration
of Healing*—5' x 4' paintings of people touched

by breast cancer. *There is more here than I can paint,*
asks me to interview the models, collect their stories.

 Georgia heat and humidity yield to chill of saffron
and scarlet. The artist packs his well-travelled

flat-bed truck—canvas and easels, paint brushes
and tooth brushes, Debussy and Miles Davis. He is

moving to Vermont to housesit his sister's lake
house for at least the winter, to paint *Metamorphosis,*

a series of butterflies. As he leaves he puts in my
hands the drawing of a woman napping on a sofa.

On the back he has written *Waking up after a long
rest! He* promises *We will talk every day.*

Lights

You left just now
tail lights glowing
down the gravel road
springs on your packed truck
joining the choir of tree frogs.
I try to deny the lump
crowding my throat
as I go through the house
turning off lights.

Intermission

I know the just-picked red pepper pod
& rosemary in your vodka, the sienna,
cadmium & charcoal in the rumples

of your hands—and still your artist's
shoulders never rotate fully open—shrouded
in paint- stained long-sleeved white shirts

you buy for four dollars at Goodwill. Zorba
dancing & the nightmares of a seven-year old
in the same ill-fitting skin & I am *just*

a young lady having Saturday breakfast with
you at Java Jive you tell the person calling
your phone. *Just a young lady*—diaphanous

robe of ancient legend exchanged for jeans
& a crisp white linen shirt. The intoxication
sweet. The price of nectar steep.

Metamorphosis

The artist neglects his promise of frequent
calls to me from Vermont. *I'm here to measure*

*my life beyond sixty, for silence to paint a series
of butterflies. You deserve better.* We talk—

snowfall, beaver dams, bear and fox tracks,
lake ice thick enough to walk on. I read him

new poems—pink calamine lotion cooling
poison ivy, my mother's hands. *You have*

to take your writing seriously. I register
for a week poetry workshop in the Georgia

mountains. New vocabulary— anaphora,
pantoum. *Describe the magnolia seed pod*

*in your hand in sixteen lines, no adverbs
or adjectives.* I mine stories of the dairy farm

where I grew up. Learning to swim in a mud-
bottomed spring-fed pond, bulls breaking

down four-railed fences, the crack of summer
lightening. Later in a weekly Atlanta workshop

I learn to shorten my poems. *No need to tell
everything you know. Leave space for the reader*

to explore. Georgia daffodils break ground,
azaleas bloom, pollen count rises. Ice cracks

on Vermont lakes. The artist packs his oil paints,
easels, sable brushes, blue jeans and Goodwill

painting shirts. I listen for the crunch of tires
along my gravel road. From the back of his

truck he hands me *Metamorphosis*—one by
one, ten paintings of butterflies each with

their caterpillar and chrysalis. Blue morph,
yellow swallow-tail, zebra, monarch. We toast

the butterflies and his return. On my kitchen
counter a white loose leaf notebook of poems—

fissures in my eight-year widow chrysalis.
The artist opens a new studio, gessoes canvas

for *Lamentations*—the impact of war on eight
women holding a babies swaddled for burial.

My raw phrases and restless clauses catch line
breaks and stanzas. *Red Clay*, my first chapbook

of poems, is published—corn on the cob fifteen
minutes from garden to table, stirring blackberry

jam, *whites only signs*. On the cover—I am
the girl in pigtails running along a farm road.

The Caribou Accords

He orders cappuccino with half and half
                      please and adds sugar
She orders decaffeinated latte with skim milk
                      medium size
They ask for real cups, no paper ones
                      with heat shields
The clerk shouts to the coffee conductor
                      skinny decaf latte
They sit in the back at a narrow table
                      with a checkerboard surface
He fiddles with his stirring stick
                      threatens to flip it
across the room as children do
                      with a fork or spoon
Places it cross-ways through the corners
                      of the checkerboard squares
Bounces it off the back
                      of her hands
Uses it as a baton, symphony maestro
                      midwife to a perfect chord.
He has diverted her from her morning walk
                      to coffee in this new place
Uncertainty spins her
                      widowed synapses
not the *if* but the *how*
                      of the relationship
She was prepared (she thought)
                      to disconnect

He'd previously argued
            she deserved better than him
this day catalogued
            his limits at nearing sixty
They talked two hours, no rancor
            of inadequacies, of aging
of fears, of breaking bread
            the energy between them
Nothing new said
            only the saying out loud
in one another's lives.

**Your Eyebrows Praise Dandelions
Gone to Seed**

Your eyes sanctify morning's
blue light
You voice fills spinnakers
with sandhill song
Your ribs shelter orphaned
Arctic calves
Your hands harmonize harpsichords
on river shoals
Your elbows fill big dippers
with cool spring water
Your knees lay tables of apple pie
and pavlova
Your toes muddle mudpies
of solstice seasons
Your feet unfurl quicksilver wings in
asteroid meadows
You pleat the aurora borealis beneath
your shoulder blades
and bring it home to me.

The Gathering

Swell upon swell   crow mob

      surge upon surge   across

the river   shadow the meadow

        congregate   jabbering

circling   hanging

    thirty or forty   I lose count

      red-tailed hawk   slopes

    in on   the thermals

        lone interloper

    greeted with   precision assaults

from above   from below

    from left   from right

      crow squads

  take turns

        dive bombing

                the screaming hawk

barred owl   lands   awkwardly

        top of the tallest   loblolly pine

     silent observer

like me   of the   ear-splitting

              brawl   of the

        hawk's   survival struggle

      Sudden

           silence   only the

fading   rabble of

                      a murder of crows

      movin' on   up   the   river.

Insurrection January 6

> *Come to Washington January 6. Be there!*
> *Will be wild! President Donald J. Trump*

I.
They come to lay waste to police barricades
and lives/   warriors with axes, knives & fists/
come to scale ramparts, shear windows/   come
prepared with maps of offices & hallway security/
come with battering rams to thunder doors/   come
in battle helmets, gas masks, hand guns & assault
rifles, bullet proof vests/   They come carrying
steel pipes & baseball bats, bull horns, tasers,
two-way radios, zip ties/   come with lumber and
rope, build a gallows and noose, chant *Lynch
the Vice President! Hang Mike Pence*/   They
climb strategic Capitol ground trees/ form military
style "sacks" through red hat mob/ parade a
Confederate flag in the Rotunda/ pose proudly in
a Camp Auschwitz t-shirt /   hunt down Senators
and House members, plunder their offices/   shout
Kill Nancy Pelosi /   weaponize fire extinguishers
& police shields /   crush a police-man in a door/
Blue Lives Matter becomes Kill police with their
own guns/   They sharpen American flagpoles into
spears/ throw a news photographer over a wall/
they replace red, white and blue American
flags over the Capitol, with blue Trump flags.

II.
Three hours into the insurrection President
of the United States Trump records a video /
We had an election stolen from us. We
love you. You are very special. Go home now.

III.
The mob leaves leave behind an inventory of dead
& injured, corridors painted in feces, stairwells
sprayed with the semen of a white American ethno-
state/ they leave Congress Members stepping
across fractured glass, footprints of blood as they
come out of hiding/ they leave interns, staff, house-
keepers, press disassembling barricades of sofas
and file cabinets/ Congressional aides bring back to
the Chamber/. three leather-strapped mahogany
boxes containing state-certified election documents.
Ten hours after the insurrection began Vice-
President Pence reconvenes the Constitutionally
mandated state-by-state Electoral College count of
the 2020 United States Presidential election.

IV.
147 Republican Members of Congress
vote common cause with their hunters

147 Republican Members
imbue the insurrection with legitimacy

147 Republican Members
seal a Faustian bargain

147 Republican Congress members
exchange their souls for a choke-hold on America

V.
3:40 AM January 7, 2021 3:40AM Vice President
Pence announces Jo Biden duly elected
President of the United States of America.

Vulcanus Eruptus

Cone of fire
magma of fear-mongers
fall lines of macerated souls
currents of conspiracy   slopes of sycophants
veins of lava lies   ventricles of ash dogma
plumes   of white acid   scalding the seas.

On Visiting an Abecedarian Atelier

    introduce yourself to the asymmetrical Aristotelian abstracts, to the bowers of badger brushes & baroque busts cast in celadon & Caucasian charcoal. Descend the staircase into deep-state doppler diptychs, easels of encaustic etchings, the finesse of fauvist frescos, grayscale gardens of delight in hate-hued horizontals. Interview iconic impasto impressionists & jaded jugglers keening for kinesthetic ring-kissing in gold & lithium landscapes. Muddle models in murals of narcissist nudes opining for Orion's belt & Old Master ombre on stary nights. Play poker, eat potatoes, pas de deux with pointillism quarks & quicksilver. Reckon a reconnaissance of radical roues, surreal screamers of trompe l'oeil, triptychs of truth under-painting in umber & ultramarine on Vemeered vellum. Water the lilies, watercolor the woodcuts. Weed the iris, whitewash xanthium xenophobes. Proof yellow yeast, zigzag zeniths of zinc. Leave the lights on.

Cast Iron Skillets

The Chattahoochee River runs rust-red as if
a dam of hundred-year-old cast-iron skillets

burst upstream drowning river banks, heaving
water up Buck Creek, swamping the nearby

meadow, splitting the bronze lid on an above-
ground concrete sewer manhole releasing a six-

foot wastewater geyser, depositing mud ten feet
high on sycamore and pine, slicing a diagonal

across the fall line in the gravel road below my house.
The river stops two hundred yards downhill

from my kitchen. A once in every five-hundred years flood,
a twelve inch cast-iron skillet on my stove.

Neely Farm

I.
Early 1930s. Frank Neely pieces together four
hundred acres along Georgia's Chattahoochee
River. Hard red clay hills, scrub pine, flooded
bottomlands. Terraces the hills to heal erosion,

drains the bottoms with a system of sub-surface
tiles, builds a prize-winning dairy herd. *Colored*
veterans return from World War II plant and harvest
corn sileage in rows straight as horizontal plumb

lines, fill three silos. *Make hay* on upland fields.
Stack alfalfa bales in barn lofts where my brothers
and I play hide and seek. Frank is our grandfather.
We call him Mimi.

II.
Cusp of winter morning. Mimi joins me along
the Chattahoochee past shoals where Native
Americans stretched weir to fish until herded
west at gun-point. Pass oaks and pines fallen
in the river—their roots given up to surges of eight-
foot water from an upstream dam. We cross Buck
Creek where my brothers and I cooled off in Georgia
summers and upstream neighbor Mr. Duncan ferried

his *finest corn likker* onto the river—avoiding
revenuers in two counties. Toll paid to Mimi *in kind*.

In the meadow we find shards of barbed wire and
rusted No Trespassing signs—reminders this was

where heifers too young to breed and milk grazed.
When Mimi turned eighty-five and I was twenty-six
he deeded this riverfront, creek and meadow to me.
(Comparable to my brothers.) Here my three children

learn to find the Big Dipper and Orion's belt in night
skies, to draw circles of light with sparklers, to set off
Big Thunder fireworks without singing hands or hair,
to practice driving figure eights in the red Ford F-100

and the Big Blue Ford 8000 tractor when legs get
long enough to reach the brakes. Now Mimi's great-
grandchildren, run kites into March meadow winds,
slip bare-foot into Buck Creek, compete for the biggest
rock-splash on one another, set race course for twigs
and leaves. First they have to drive past the Mallard
logo of the Neely Farm subdivision and three hundred
mailboxes with identical Black horseheads.

III.
I climb the worn red kitchen stepstool, take down
the last flask of Mr. Duncan's *finest corn likker,*
describe to my grandfather the smell of Georgia earth
as diesel as bulldozers slice verdant pastures and

fertile fields into streets. Thuds, dust clouds as barns,
silos, white-washed fences fall. I want to ask Mimi if
families sold him their *home places* in order to feed
their families in times of no jobs and bread-lines.

I wipe off the bottle of *corn likker,* pour a shot,
share it with my grandfather.   We call him Mimi.

Pick-up Sticks

Tree trunks and limbs
        splayed across the forest floor, clear-cut
        sixty foot pick-up-sticks—pine, hundred-
        year-old oaks, a beech carved with a heart.

Root balls
        wrenched from Georgia's red earth—
        twelve and twenty feet in diameter,
        tangled like Medusa's crown of snakes.

Understory
        shoved into ten-foot banks—redbud,
        buckeye, maple and dogwood, wild rose
        briars, flame azaleas and squirrels' nests.

Night path of a shy sandy fox
        spring carpets of chanterelles, mayapples,
        bloodroot and trillium. swallowed
        in mosaics of bulldozer tracks .

Doe and spotted fawn
        white tails up, thread their way through
        the pick-up sticks, forage for acorns
        on this bare unfamiliar hill.

The hammer of piliated woodpeckers
        silenced as are red-tailed hawks teaching
        fledgling to fly and barred owls calling
        who cooks for you, across the dark night.

Along Buck Creek

Rain & wind leave a chaos of fallen trees &
tangled limbs, dams of branches, neon yellow
tennis balls, deflated soccer balls, fresh eddies
& new beaches, a volunteer cluster of Lilies
of the Valley, a Canada goose nest
sheltered among tree roots with five eggs
along Buck Creek

mysterious kill-off of microscopic crayfish &
minnows, a deer carcass abandoned
by coyotes, rancid bloody limbs, a congregation
of flies in the eye holes, marijuana & bongs stashed
under the lip of the creek that once went dry
along Buck Creek

a steel pipe crosses the creek—transit line
for suburban waste
a table & lean-to shed spray-painted & carved
with anti-sematic & racist icons—
hang man cartoons   KKK
a man hanging from a cross with two tears
oven at 4500 degrees, four people in it—
one a child cries *help*
along Buck Creek

twenty foot magnolia grandiflora planted
at birth of my oldest grandchild   today the two

youngest pick King Alfred daffodils
planted by the grandfather they never knew
clutch them in their hands
home to their mother—daughter
of the man who planted them
forty-five years ago on the hillside
overlooking Buck Creek.

Seven Days in Spring

Day One.   Lenten roses congregate in our front garden. Japanese maples dip into the gutters. Crab apple blooms scarlet along the driveway. Rubber bands of tightness across your chest. You try to lie down in the guest room *No! No! It's different than when I had a heart attack before. Honest!* A wren begins to build her nest on our bedroom porch.

Day Two. Emergency Rooms overflow into parking lots with Covid patients. *Risks outweigh going to the hospital as long as fever and oxygen levels normal. Remain isolated. Wear masks, wash your hands the time it takes to sing Happy Birthday twice.* The terracotta woman from my grandparents' garden oversees the unexpected return of a ruby petunia.

Day Three. I continue confused as to the distinction between *isolate* and *quarantine*, scour kitchen counters with Clorox wipes. Scrub keyboards, phones, TV remotes, handles on doors. Discover *sanitize* settings on the dishwasher and washing machine. Reacquaint myself with an old prescription of an anti-anxiety drug. I pick the first daffodils of spring.

Day Four. Your temperature and oxygen levels remain normal. I arrange grocery delivery, make chicken soup with carrots, onions, fennel and garlic, put on a mask, bring a bowl and spoon to the guest room. You blow me air-kisses from behind your blue mask. The wren continues nest-building. No eggs.

Day Five. Spring storms flood the nearby meadow, leave pine-pollen-yellow flotsam and jetsam, slippery mud-plastered winter grass and a red stomp rocket. You play solitaire on the I-pad, fall asleep with it across your chest. Your snoring is music.

Day Six. Today is your birthday. I bake your favorite scratch oatmeal raisin cookies. Grandchildren giggle, roll downhill in overgrown yard grass, congregate at the guestroom window. They sing raucous *Happy Birthday* to you their Pap Pap! A squirrel claims squatter's rights to the blue bird house, suns its face through the hole.

Day Seven. You reassert control of the television remote. We sit masked-up six feet apart in the living room, cheer for favorites on The Great British Baking Show. Finish the Ben and Jerry's Chunky Monkey a neighbor left by our kitchen door. You made your favorite lunch today—canned pork and beans, crackers with peanut butter and raisins. You put your plate in the dishwasher. Five eggs in the wren's nest.

Melancholia Covida

I wake exhausted after intense and vivid dreams
Covid dreams even if not about Covid. Aim

an instant thermometer at my forehead like
a gun. No fever. Shower hoping to scrub

the sadness away, accomplish only a reminder
we are out of soap. Excavate heaps of laundry

for clean underwear. Excavate the kitchen sink
for a coffee mug. Ignore unpaid bills spilling

onto the mudroom floor along with coupons
for gutters and riding lawn mowers. Clocks

read Salvador Dali time. Check newspaper
mastheads for day of the week. Rescued dogs

need rabies shots. Geraniums and marigolds
need deadheading Hair needs cutting, teeth

need cleaning.   Last night I burned couscous
in my favorite pot.   Twenty miles away Rayshard

Brooks, a Black man, is murdered with a police
gun in a Wendy's parking lot. I want to stop

counting Black men killed by police. I want
to sleep under a Gee's Bend quilt. I want

Leonard Cohen to *gather me in*. I want asparagus
in the refrigerator not to be rotten.

Contagion

Who among us has not been infected
with COVID fear?   Waking, wanting
to vomit but the vomit hangs burning
in our esophagus and we are not certain
of the day of the week or when our toilet
paper will run out and if there will be more
in the stores. Who among us does not fear
dying alone, COVID keeping loved ones
distant   unlike when my children and
I held their father's hands and feet keeping
rhythm with his damaged heart and shallow
breaths   until   there   were   none   left.

These Covid days and nights hazmat-faced
doctors, frayed-thin nurses and respiratory
therapists stand in as on a computer screen
their patient is reassured by loved ones' voices

> *Of course, we will remember your*
> *mother's November birthday and*
> *the dog's monthly heartworm pills.*
>
> *Yes, we will make certain your*
> *grandfather's gold pocket watch*
> *goes to his eldest great-grandson.*

Who among us has not rehearsed permission-giving?
> *It is okay for you to go.*
> *We will all be fine.*

Who among us has not practiced remembering the faces of loved ones?

Through the Lens of Dorthea Lange's Camera

A woman in the Community Food Bank
walks past bins of frozen turkeys
pyramids of pumpkins
Her fingers drift across plastic bags
of cranberries and marshmallows
Linger for a handful of green beans
two sweet potatoes, two rolls of toilet paper
a loaf of Colonial white bread
She pulls her threadbare gray jacket tight
to her chest, walks half- mile
to her cardboard shelter and bedroll
pleated under the Interstate 75 bridge
     no kitchen   no oven
     no over the river and through the woods
in the grayscale lens
of Dorthea Lange's Graflex camera.

Fog

The fog comes in on little cat
feet swallowing shallow creeks

curves in mountain roads
roiling sheaves of wheat

grasslands, coastal plains
hesitating over harbors, cities

a red cardinal curls passerine feet
on winter limbs of a native azalea

black sunflower seed in his stout beak
turns his crested head left   then right

back left again   certain spring will
come   the azalea will flame boughs

of double-fisted orange and yellow
blossoms   the fog will move on.

Petition

Consecrate first sprigs of hair after chemotherapy
the Pope washing and kissing prisoners' feet
Michigan plumbers replacing lead water pipes
Harriet Tubman's railroad schedule

Hallow Harriet Tubman's railroad schedule
thin arms of nameless children firing AK-47s
hands and fingers of children in sweat shops
Ruby Bridges buckling her patent leather shoes

Sanctify Ruby Bridges buckling her shoes
John Lewis preaching *good trouble*
Marian Anderson's Lincoln Memorial contralto
the voices of Malala Yousafzai and Greta Thunberg

Praise the firestorm voices of Malala and Greta
Chef José Andrés' World Wide Kitchens
my suffragette great-grandmother on her way to jail
Robert Frost inviting us on *the road less travelled*
    and that has made all the difference.

Catching Air Before the Shoals

I watch the current slip-slide side to side
a woman swims below the surface
teaching her daughter to stroke
with the lap of the water
secure in unfamiliar currents
alongside otters and minnows
and ruts left by beavers dragging trees
into the river to float
downstream for lodge building
teaching her daughter to let the water hold her
catching air just before the shoals
her powerful body shimmering in
the spill of sunset shadows
in the water's afternoon chill
her black hair opalescent
She floats on her back
the water her guide, her pillow
her song to the herons and kingfishers
to the snakes and turtles and alligators
to pine tree branches
splintering the water's surface
I envy the easy stroke of this woman
swimming downstream, turning upstream
embracing the current, her shoulders, her legs
and arms cut silently into the water like weeds
She does not need to breathe.

Tree

I am tree
silhouette in winter
harbinger of redbud spring
blossoming crabapple on the meadow's edge
full figured summer—my harvest
sweet pears and hard tart quince
I am locust posts anchoring fences
hickory canes steadying walkers
limbs embracing children's swings
> *How do you like to go up in a swing,*
> *Up in the air so blue?*

My cambium layer delicate, fragile
I can be transplanted when care is taken
I bloom an allee of magnolia grandiflora
I draw lightening
I dislike old saws
my age measured in rings
I bear *strange fruit*
> *Blood on the leaves and blood at the root*

I am not tree
no ancestors ancient as centenarian oaks
no redwoods and sequoias measuring
height by closeness to the moon
no capacity for photosynthesis
nor for washing carbon dioxide

I do not grow moss on my northern side
I cannot be turned into legs of a Stickley table
or milled for an Amish barn
I have no leaves to hold up the stars
In death the tree and I are one
in a box of plain pine
comforted by moist earth
and the rains of spring.

You can't be suspicious of a tree,
or accuse a bird or a squirrel of subversion
or challenge the ideology of a violet.

Hal Borland *Spring is For Laughter,* 1952

Notes

What to Believe
December 14, 2012 Twenty children between six and seven and six adults murdered in Sandy Hook Elementary, Newtown, Connecticut by a twenty year old man with guns legally purchased by his mother whom he killed first. Bushmaster XM15-E2S, Glock 20SF handgun, .22LR Savage Mark II bolt-action rifle.

Witness
Blood and soil. A nationalist slogan expressing Nazi Germany's ideal of a racially defined national body (blood) united with a settlement area (soil).

Without Sanctuary available in book form and on the Without Sanctuary website. The collection will be permanently housed at the National Center for Civil and Human Rights in Atlanta.

Petition
Malala Yousafzai. At fifteen survived shots in the head by the Taliban. *I am stronger than fear.* Pakistani activist for female education, Nobel Peace Prize.

Greta Thunberg. Began her advocacy at fifteen. *On climate change, we have to acknowledge we have failed.* Swedish environmental activist with Asperger's and long blonde braids, known for challenging world leaders to take immediate action for climate change mitigation.

Acknowledgments

The bookends of *Corn Likker & Daffodils* belong to Cecilia Woloch mentor to a beginning poet twenty years ago who cut me no slack and to Jeffrey Levine at Tupelo Press critical reader of this manuscript who celebrated some of the poems and encouraged me to let some others rest. Thank you zoom for stepping into the covid breach. I've "met" a catalogue of extraordinary poets and friends through readings and webinars and tutorials and workshops on line. Thank you poets Pam, Merna, Carolyn and Lisa for our monthly critiques and laughter. Thank you to the following for publishing versions of poems from *Corn Likker & Daffodils*. *Bellevue Literary Review, Banyan Review, Fauxmoir Literary Review, Grande Dame Literary, Half and One, Quibble Lit, The Write Launch*. And most of all to Sal my life partner and first listener to every line—after our rescue dogs Angus and Bailey lose interest.

Eve Hoffman

Storyteller and poet Eve Hoffman grew up on a Georgia dairy farm. Still seeks dirt roads and Guernsey cream. Her lineage includes a Revolutionary War soldier, a mill owner "hanged near to death" by Yankees, a suffragette leader and a grandfather who helped shape the south as chairman of the regional Federal Reserve Bank. She's been called a provocateur. Her personal and political lives not tidily separated. Honored as a "Remarkable Woman" by her alma mater Smith College. Full-length *Memory & Complicity* published by Mercer University Press nominated for Georgia poetry author of the year. Chapbooks: *Red Clay* and *SHE*. Art/narrative: *A Celebration of Healing—twenty-one lives impacted by breast cancer.* evehoffmanpoet.com
Contact: evehoffmanassistant@gmail.com

www.ingramcontent.com/pod-product-compliance
Lightning Source LLC
Chambersburg PA
CBHW030057170426
43197CB00010B/1562